WHAT THEY CAN'T SEE AFFECTS THEM

SHAMIKA KING

What They Can't See Affects Them

Published by Nourish Inspirations, LLC

Copyright © 2019 by Shamika King.

ISBN No. 9781793259356

Table of Contents

Acknowledgements

First and foremost, All Glory and Honor to my Heavenly Father God.

Thank you for creating me and filling me up with your Wisdom, Clarity, Understanding and Knowledge; not only for myself, yet for those who are willing; not by force, to receive from you through the strong vessel you've implanted within me. Father God, without you I am nothing but with you I am everything and more.

I am the vine, you are the branches. He who abides in Me, and I in him, bears much fruit; for without Me you can do nothing.

John 15:5 NKJV

Train up a child in the way he should go, And when he is old, he will not depart from it.

Proverbs 22:6 NKJV

Chapter 1: Communication

Just like every other chapter in this book, this one is important. Communication is not only consequential but it's a necessity. Without this essential, life can be façade and arduous. As we all know communication starts at home. Now just because it starts at home doesn't necessarily means it was learned or occurred there.

If it was, that's great. If it wasn't, as a child it wasn't our fault that most of our parents lacked teaching us. Most of our parents probably didn't know how. To make matters worse they refused to learn for our sakes. Once again, this is not our fault. It was a requisite that our parents declined to provide. What happens when we grow into adults and decide to have children that yearns for this same essential?

Well, there is a possibility that one or two things will occur.

1. *We do what we've been taught by actions (which is confusing to the child) and we pass down the aberrant way of communication.*
2. *We learn for ourselves first, the proper way to communicate. We then, break the anomalous cycle of communication for our children's sake.*

It is important for us to know that what our parents chose to do should not affect how we choose to live. It should not affect or get in the way of how we raise our children in this time of day. However, majority of us have allowed this affection to creep in and take its course permanently in our lives. If this is what you choose then so be it. You have free will to do as you please, yet this is not fair to your children. The same things that you saw, didn't see and didn't receive that affected you, may be the same things that affect your children.

Moving forward, I would like to further explain this inarticulate killer when it's not learned called communication. I'm not sure if you were ever aware but there are *4 malfunctional ways that most of us communicate.*

1. *Assumptions*
2. *Discrimination*
3. *Actions*
4. *Talking at and demanding*

Assumptions

We assume someone is angry because they're frowning. We never think that maybe the individual is in deep thought about something. Their thoughts could be unintentionally forming their face expression without them having a clue. However, we don't try to approach the individual by communicating, to see if that's really the case. We assume, predict, and leave it alone. We really believe we have it all figured out too, until later down the line when the real facts come about.

Discrimination

Most of us discriminate to the extreme. We try to act like we don't, but we do and it's so unfair. We go off looks, rumors, and/or a bad life experience/background. We treat everyone the same or different without first communicating. It's not that we're afraid to approach and have compassion for others. It's just that most of us don't know how and so we take the easy way out. We'd rather find out through someone else about somebody else, instead of getting to know the individual for ourselves. I guess when it's all said and done, you can't do something you don't know how to do unless you try to put the effort in doing so. Nowadays putting effort in anything is too much pressure for most of us. Instead of taking a stand, we'd rather settle on the stand and proceed with discriminating.

Actions

We show by our actions almost everything. We also learn what we think we know, by another individual actions. By doing this, one or two things can occur. Someone or we ourselves can misinterpret whatever is being shown instead of communicated. I understand that actions speak louder than words. However, what I have a hard time

3

understanding is how most of us use actions before words. At least say what you mean then let your actions back it up. Most of us don't say anything and we expect people to use common sense. This is so unprofessional, confusing and unfair. Not everyone activates their sense to understand what you may believe is common. What if the other individual happens to be unaware of what's occurring?

For Example: Let's just say you work Monday-Friday only. Friday evening before ending your shift, you noticed that the weekend shifts would be short staff. You heard your boss loudly complaining about it but since he didn't come to you directly, you didn't worry about it. Saturday morning, your off day arrives. Your boss calls you, yelling through the phone asking why you're not at work. You explain to him that he never asked you to come in on your off day. He figures that since you saw him by action, yelling and complaining, you'd use your common sense and come to work.

If this is not the craziest, discombobulated way of communication, I'm not sure what is. However, this was just an example. I wanted to give you a better outlook on how most of us operate with our actions daily. To make matters worse, most of us say "I'm grown I don't owe anyone an explanation." Now that may be true to a certain instinct but that's not the case. The fact of the matter is that yes, we're all grown yet we don't know how to elucidate.

Talking at and Demanding

We talk at people selfishly demanding what we say to be considered. It doesn't matter what the other person thinks, feel, or may want to suggest. It's our way or the highway and all hell will break loose if anybody should disagree. This is how most of us communicate. It's solipsism and unethical. It doesn't teach others or our children how to be open-minded and expressive at all. It teaches them how to isolate themselves and secrete their inner turmoil.

This also structures a rooted foundation of fear inside of them. It causes them to stay in a devastating situation periodically. They will do anything to satisfy others, still feeling worthless, unsatisfied and used. This type of communication may even lead to suicidal thoughts. It may make your children or others feel like their presence is a mistake.

I'm sure you know someone like this or it may even be you. Looking from the outside in, people would frame this as being a coward. I understand this well enough to see that it's the adjusting in being talked at and demanded, permanently in one's life. When we talk at our children and demand them to do any and everything in most cases, it damages them. It causes most of them to grow into disrespectful and self-centered adults.

They're constantly on a run doing everything yet feeling like everything they do will never be enough. They live on not knowing how to properly communicate while mocking others who do. They sometimes would rather not communicate at all because they can't control this form of communication that they've become immune to.

Moving forward, I would like to explain the *3 proper ways of communication*.

1. *Talk to*
2. *Listen*
3. *Understand*

Talk to

When we set our fears and assumptions aside, we welcome proper communication in unimaginable ways. As we talk to others compassionately and patiently, we make them feel secured. Not only do they comprehend what we're saying, but they pick up a familiarity in the spirit. It's as if we're speaking to that area deep within them. Although they can't see it, doesn't mean it's not there.

When we talk to them, they trust us enough to share that unseen infection that's been lingering for years. How you talk to a person is substantial. It calms the individual down. It helps them break free from the many things hidden beneath the surface. A lot of people walk around ashamed of their imperfections and testimonies. They've concluded that no one will ever understand. In most cases, some people will or won't understand, either way it's still best to ventilate.

A lot of us have never been talked to, we've been talked at. This is the cause of most of us not knowing what it's like to properly communicate. All we know is how to receive and bare the burden. For majority of us, we think that being talked at and baring the burden is a sign of strength, however, it's a sign of weakness. Manumitting is a sign of strength, which is why when we're talked to, we feel much more redeemed.

Listen

How did it make you feel when your parents failed to listen to you? It can be overwhelming trying to explain the simplest thing to a person who refuse to listen. Most of our parents are adjusted to being independent and self-centered. In this case, it's difficult trying to get them to listen. It was probably never taught to them and so to them, there is no point in wasting time trying to teach their children. They simply know what they know. It's impossible to get them to open what they've put on a limit.

For some parents, listening is a fear. You may say or ask them something, in which, they don't know. The problem is not about what they don't know, it's about them being afraid to listen and gain knowledge. I'm sure we've all heard the saying "what you don't know, won't hurt you." I'm sure our parents have as well, which explains why most of them left us not knowing many things that would've been beneficial. In my opinion, I believe what you don't know will hurt you, not right away but in the long run.

To listen means to be held accountable. A lot of us can't stand listening because we know after what we've heard, we become accountable for it. No one wants to be accountable for anything. Being held accountable opens the door for responsibility and nowadays for most of us, that's just too much.

Take a moment and read over what most of us fail to realize when it comes to listening.

- *Our children respect what we have to say more than rare, and they grow and gain knowledge nonstop.*
- *It benefits not only us as parents but our children as well.*
- *Our children are more open to speak up, no matter the situation.*
- *The burden of fear is lifted from us parents. The lack of knowledge and generational dysfunction no longer spreads.*
- *We will no longer run away from being held accountable and taking care of our responsibilities.*

Now try to imagine if the parent and child refused to listen. Neither one would reap the benefits from listening. If you look around in most environments, no one listens. If you look deeper you can spot the lack of respect, effort, accountability, and responsibility. Although listening takes a lot of effort, the more it's practiced, the more it will improve.

Being raised by parents who probably never listened to you, or never thought to teach you how to listen, may be overwhelming. I know you're probably wondering; how do you listen? Before giving some helpful tips, I just want you to know the ability for you to listen is possible. You're already equipped to do it, however, as a parent it takes consistency, patience, and practice.

- *Be completely quiet when your child or anyone else is speaking.*
- *Give direct eye contact. This shows that whatever is being discussed is very important to you.*
- *Once your child or other individual is completely done speaking, see if it's alright to give feedback. I say this because not everyone want feedback, they just want to be heard and understood.*
- *Always repeat what was stated, then ask questions compassionately. This is just so that there's no misunderstanding on what's being discussed.*

As you continue to read thoroughly through this book, you will learn that everything I speak on starts at home first. Whatever takes place on the inside will eventually begin to reproduce on the outside. Most of us, as parents and majority of our children don't listen because we never experienced what it felt like to be talked to.

This explains why, most of us are quick to get on defense mode, offended, or feel intimidated. Rarely do we listen thoroughly over what's being said.

Understand

Although communication is very substantial without understanding it doesn't make sense. When you're dealing with your children, it is important to build an understanding relationship. A lack of comprehension may confuse your child and hold them back tremendously. Without an understanding of what's being talked about and heard, communication will repeat its dysfunctional cycle.

In order to properly communicate you must talk to, listen and understand. You can't do one without the other. In this time of day, a lot of us parents are mixing the maladjusted and proper way of communication together.

Children reproduce what they see their parents produce. Try to be aware because they will soak up everything like a sponge just to squeeze it out later in life. Most parents talk at and demand yet never listen. Most parents think they understand by assumptions. Most parents use their actions to speak, but never talk to their children.

This may cause confusion within the child. This may also lead them down a road of delusion, while lacking knowledge of proper communication. All it takes is time and patience to teach your children how to properly communicate. It's not going to happen overnight. It's a never-ending learning process and the more it's practiced, the better it will become.

Start off each day with just a small amount of proper communication. It can be at any time of the day.

For example: When you pick your children up from school, talk to them. Ask them questions regarding their day. Listen, understand, then talk again. Understanding is not only a comprehension of what's being communicated. It's a level of respect for what may not always be agreed on. The more your children grow, the more you will learn new things about them and vice versa, as you properly communicate.

There's a possibility that this may not be something you were raised doing. It might've never been taught or practiced with you as a child. That's alright because it doesn't have to stop there. Based off the wisdom that I'm sharing with you. If you should agree and receive, you will gain the knowledge needed to practice the proper way of communication for your child's sake.

Chapter 2: Discipline

Look around you, take a walk in your neighborhood, go for a ride on the bus/car or simply turn on the TV. I'm sure you've done it all, however, I have 3 questions for you to think about.

- *What is Respect?*
- *Where does it comes from?*
- *Are you teaching your children the importance of morals?*

I believe that respect comes from the inside. If you don't respect yourself, it's impossible for you to respect anyone else. More than rare, I hear a lot of people yelling so desperately, that in order to give respect, it should be given first. So, this means that if you want to be respected someone must give it first, before you decide to release it.

I'm starting to believe we make up our own way of doing things, then force ourselves to believe it. In my opinion, this is the craziest outlook of respect that I've ever heard and seen.

For Example: This is like you telling your boss, for you to come to work, he or she needs to call and ask you first. Doesn't this sound crazy? You should already be consistent knowing that whether your boss calls you or not, it's your responsibility to be at work everyday on time. In the same way, respect should be handled like this.

Whether we receive it or not, it should be given freely. It should be given freely to those who disrespect us as well. Would it benefit us to only respect those who respect us? No, it wouldn't. Why? Because they already know how to respect. It would benefit and teach those who don't know. It would teach others that they don't have to wait to be respected to show respect.

To be honest, respect is taught through discipline. Growing up, if you ever been disciplined, then you should know how to respect others as well as you respect yourself. Reading up to this point. Stop and ask yourself, are your children disciplined? Just like communication, discipline starts at home. The things that you do in front and behind your child is very important.

Please don't force yourself to believe that what you do behind your child won't affect them. They may not know exactly what you're doing, but they can feel the tension. They can also sense the negativity, pick up on your energy and begin to reciprocate it. Things you say and partake in, such as; drama, profanity, explicit conversations, and overrated arguments it all affects your child. If you're not careful with properly disciplining your child, they will reproduce in the environment what's been planted at home.

When your child has not been disciplined, they unintentionally show it. The disrespect and lack of knowledge manifest naturally, whether they're with you or someone else.

For Example: I'm sure you've been on the bus or anywhere in general and witnessed children of all ages act very ignorant and disrespectful. I'm sure you've witnessed children falling out on the ground screaming because they can't have their way. Fighting their parents and/or grandparents or using profanity towards them. This may have been you growing up. It may even be your child, or it may be someone you know or don't know.

Bystanders and those around that are in the act of being humiliated don't address the issue at all. To be completely honest, it's not their responsibility. Nowadays, most parents will get on defense mode if you stop their child from disrespecting you or them. It's just safe to not say anything at all. It's crazy and makes no sense. When you see children acting out of character like this, it's because they're not being disciplined.

A lot of us are grown and have become parents ourselves. We've either grew up being disciplined, grew up with our parents as our friends, or grew up being handed everything but morals. Moving forward, I would like to explain the causes and effects of the three.

Growing up under a roof with morals yet not much materialistic things is very healthy for the parent and the child. This will bring peace to everyone in the household, not perfection. It's never about what you have that matters, it's always about what you'll never run out of. If you teach your child about what comes priceless in life, you'll have no worries and your heart will be glad.

Discipline your children, and they will give you peace of mind and will make your heart glad.

-Proverbs 29:17 NLT

Growing up with your parents as your friend; smoking, drinking, cursing, clubbing, competition and jealousy, is not healthy at all. Now if your friendship doesn't come between the respect you have with your child and vice versa, then that's fine. It's only unhealthy when you're more of a friend, than you are a parent. There may come a time when you try to discipline your child and they may fail to respect you, due to it never being taught.

To discipline a child produces wisdom, but a mother is disgraced by an undisciplined child.

-Proverbs 29:15NLT

Growing up being handed everything under the sun except discipline is unhealthy. Your child will feel as if life is all about whatever they want it to be. Wrong or right, they will feel that they can do, say, go and come as they please. We see and hear about a lot of these kind of people today. They were once spoiled children, now all grown up.

They may be either imprisoned, addicted to drugs/alcohol, murdering others for whatever reason, prideful, leeching off others to take care of them, careless about life, or secretly bombing the world. They do things like this simply because they want what they want. They feel it should be given because they've always been handed it, yet, stopped receiving it. You would think it's the people whose been raised and haven't been handed everything. In most cases, it's both, but majority of the time it's the children that's been handed everything.

A servant pampered from childhood will become a rebel.

-Proverbs 29:21NLT

After the child becomes adjusted to discipline, it will be installed forever. It will flow naturally wherever they go, and they will be glad to accept discipline from their parents or others.

A wise child accepts a parent's discipline; a mocker refuses to listen to correction.

-Proverbs 13:1NLT

I understand that disciplining your child can be overwhelming. I know that you love your child so much, maybe even a bit too much. This may cause you to contemplate when it comes to discipling them. When I say discipline, I'm not only referring to whooping and punishing. That's just the icing on the cake, yet that doesn't fully complete the definition of discipline. Discipline requires a lot of your time. It's more than just a pop on the hand and constantly repeating "Stop! Don't do that!" or "Stop! Stay away from that!". You have to repeatedly teach your child until they're out on their own. You have to guide them the best way possible, in the process of teaching them. Explain to them what it means to listen after you've shown them. Prepare your children to step out into the world to not only make a difference but to be different.

Repeatedly teach them morals and explain to them what consequences are and how it comes about. Everything that you learn share it with them. This will help them understand and be aware of certain signs, schemes, and manipulative people. Whatever it is that you know how to do, teach them how to do it as well. They may not need to know these things now but one day they will. It will all be very beneficial for them. You may not be with them forever but everything you teach them will.

Be sure to encourage them whenever you have the chance to, or whenever it crosses your mind to do so. Express to them how capable and successful they are even if they fail from time to time. Be sure to thank them and express your appreciation towards them for simply existing. In everything you do, have patience with your children. This will teach them to take their time with themselves as well as with others.

Try not to think that since your child is young, they don't need to know what's going on around them. It's never too early to start discipling your child. The last thing you want to experience is your child all grown up yet mocks discipline.

Those who spare the rod of discipline hate their children. Those who love their children care enough to discipline them.

-Proverbs 13:24NLT

Balance out the way you discipline your children. Don't do too much but just enough. I will better explain what I mean by this further in the book. Keep in mind that too much of anything will damage or maybe even kill an individual. As a parent, let them be a child and live a child's life.

Remain steadfast and fortified when it's time to discipline them. Once more, discipline is not strictly whooping and punishing the child. It's morals, wisdom, guidance, understanding, patience, compassion, listening, knowledge and teaching perpetually.

Chapter 3: Responsibility

Are you teaching your children how to be responsible or are you teaching them how to be irresponsible? I understand that your baby can be so precious and pure. I understand that as a parent your child will always be your baby in your eyes, but this isn't the problem. The problem is that you've allowed your baby to remain a baby while blocking their ability to grow. This may cause your child to become lost as they grow into an adult.

They may be grown still acting childish, refusing to let go of childish tendencies. This happens when they become adjusted to being treated like a child majority of their life. This also occurs when the parent does everything for the child and procrastinate when it comes to letting them take on responsibilities.

When I was a child, I spoke as a child, I understood as a child, I thought as a child; but when I became a man, I put away childish things.

– 1 Corinthians 13:11NKJV

The child may become more and more unaware of what, when, where and how to take on any task, minor or major. They may refuse to be held accountable for anything they partake in. When conflict occurs, they may always run to you. Sometimes they may make themselves feel justified and blame you for something you knew nothing about. Why? Because you've always took on their responsibilities and defended their actions, right or wrong. This is what happens when you'd rather bare the burden for your child than to teach them how to be accountable for their own actions and decision-making.

For Example: I remember when my oldest son turned one year old. He did something that caught me by surprise. He got up from crawling and walked down the hallway. I was so excited, I couldn't believe that my baby took his first steps. Now seeing that he's my son and would someday be a man, I couldn't allow myself to get overly excited.

I say this because I would've allowed myself to walk for him to the point where he felt no need. This would have caused him to return to crawling for an extended time. From that day forward, I watched as he exceeded in his walking skills. It was to the point where he started running and jumping. There were times where he fell and hurt himself, however, if he wasn't screaming with blood bursting everywhere, I didn't react.

If I was to react every time he fell, I may have hindered his growth. He wouldn't be able to understand what it's like to fall, get up and try again. Around this time a lot of people would say "He's just a baby, don't be so hard on him". I wasn't hard on him. Whenever he showed me, he was ready to exceed in a new level of growth, I got out of his way. I supported him just enough not to mutilate him. Those same people would've been calling my son a lazy monster, if I would've raised him differently. I know you're probably like that's a bit early to be teaching a child anything about responsibility. In my opinion, the earlier you start, the better it will turn out for your child.

If you look around today there are many grown men and women either shacked up with one another, or still at home with their parents. Why? Because in most cases they are afraid of taking on any kind of responsibility alone. They'd rather do it together to have someone near, to place the blame on if things don't go as they planned. Don't get me wrong, there is absolutely nothing wrong with two people helping one another. However, that's totally different from two people leeching off one another just so they won't be held accountable for anything.

You would think the people who are shacked up and leeching off one another are responsible, based off how they handle things together. Truth of the matter is, most of these men and women growth was hindered at some point during their childhood. If you ever caught them alone, you would see that it may be difficult for them to cope. Stepping outside their comfort zone to be introduced to any form of responsibility may be too much pressure.

Most of these men and women are us or our children. As a parent, after years of crippling your child it becomes draining. There comes a time where you look at your child or young adult and you're like "It's time to clean up, get a job, and move out". However, over the course of time you've become blinded. You failed to teach your child about the very things that are now stressing you out and silently affecting them. At this point there is nothing left for you to do except, get out of the way. I know this may leave you feeling guilty for your child seeing that they are not equipped to be on their own.

You probably wouldn't believe me but there are parents who are afraid to let their children live. They feel like their children will be lost without them. It's amazing to me because while they're with them, their children are still lost with them. Why? Because nothing is being taught and nothing is being learned. In most cases, this can be resolved. In other cases, it's best being left alone. Next time around try to examine the consequences first.

Most children resent their parents and blame them for everything. Other children grow old, let the hurt go and raise their children better. As parents, we all make mistakes and lack in numerous areas. This is not bad at all, there's still hope. This will give your children an opportunity to learn from what you didn't do. They may also improve in that area by overcoming and succeeding in it. Once your child is grown and out, give them distance. Pray that they seek God for wisdom, guidance and understanding.

If they choose to continue to run away from responsibility there's nothing you can do. If they refuse to be held accountable for their actions, there's nothing further that you can do. Once they are grown, they are held responsible for themselves whether they want to accept it or not.

For we are each responsible for our own conduct. -Galatians 6:5NLT

I understand as parents we just want to see our children prosper and achieve in life. It's natural for us to want what's best for our children. Let us make sure that we're not doing too much to the point where we get in their way. Let us do just enough and allow them to live their lives. We, then, won't have to worry yet we'll be at peace because we know that we've trained them properly.

Direct your child onto the right path, and when they are older, they will not leave it. -Proverbs 22:6NLT

I come to realize that most of us only fear the unknown because we're unaware of what the unknown holds. In other words, we're afraid to let our children practice being responsible because we know they aren't prepared. Truth of the matter is, they aren't prepared because most of us parents are never ready. Most of us fail to realize in order to be ready for something, you first, have to give it a try.

As parents, we have to understand that it starts with us first. It's too late in the day to be sitting around procrastinating. For an extended time, most of us have been pointing the finger in the wrong direction. It's timeout for making our children suffer and reciprocate the mistakes our parents did to us. We've failed to realize that the big picture has always been staring us in the face, hoping that we would someday understand.

They heard the alarm but ignored it, so the responsibility is theirs. If they had listened to the warning, they could have saved their lives.

-Ezekiel 33:5NLT

Most of us lack knowledge due to our past childhood, yet we rebuke knowledge for the sake of our children. It damages our children and they begin to repeat and release the dysfunctional cycle. When we hold on to past hurtful memories, we become blinded and it becomes a normal for us. We begin to feel numb and start living their life, instead of teaching them how to be responsible to live their own lives.

Although our children come from us, they don't belong to us. God created them just as well as he created us, to fulfill his purpose. We have a life and assignment, so does our children. Once again, it's not our responsibility to live for them. It's our responsibility to teach them how to be responsible in every area. It's our responsibility to prepare them to live their own life properly.

Their responsibility is to equip God's people to do his work and build up the church, the body of Christ.

-Ephesians 4:12NLT

Try to understand that although time waits on no one, it gives everyone numerous opportunities. It's never too late to restart and rectify your children. It's never too late to grasp hold of knowledge for yourself and for the sake of your children. When you see that your child is ready for something new that will benefit their growth, try not to ignore the minor things yet act accordingly.

Those minor things that most of us ignore, helps the child grow and will become major someday. They will manifest into a necessity that your child will yearn for. To help your child become responsible pay close attention to them and balance out your support for them.

Chapter 4: Difference

If you look at your children today, can you notice the distinctness about them? If you look at yourself not only as a parent but a brother and/or sister, what makes your diverseness unique? How are you different from not only your siblings but everyone that surrounds you?

There are so many things to think about when it comes to you. However, there has never seem to be enough time set aside for you to examine yourself. Perhaps you spent majority of your childhood years taking care and analyzing your siblings, wondering if not saying, "Who do you think you are? Oh, I can do that too. You ain't no better. Mama and daddy always let her/him get away with everything."

At some point in your life, your parents treated you and your siblings the same. When I say the same, I mean treated you as if you're no different. They dressed you alike and even brought you the same things. I'm sure they did this to prevent signs of favoritism or to prevent you from feeling neglected. However, most of our parents failed to realize that we still felt confused, neglected and frustrated.

For most of us, this causes us to grow distant from our family. The tension of jealousy and shade is in the air when most of us come together with our family. At times its just best to stay away and come around every so often. Although it shouldn't be like this, it has to be and its simply because of our differences. It's not much to explain because either way you'll be misunderstood and even more irritated all because you're not one in the same.

For Example: I'm sure at some point in our life we've all had a conversation with a family member. It could've been about anything, yet the smallest simplest things show how people really feel about you. During the conversation, most of us heard; "Are you stupid? Why would you do that? How you gone tell me, I been there and done that already? You ain't no better. Listen you need to do it like me, that's the only way it's gone work. If you do it your way, it will never work."

In person if we ever went to an outing with family or even close friends, I'm sure most of us heard; "Why would you wear that? That doesn't fit you. You done changed your hair again, that style is not for you." We have heard almost every negative comment. Rarely do most of us hear positive comments regarding who we are and what we do for ourselves. This explains why everyone is trying to be everyone else. It's much easier and it lowers the pressure.

It's not that you're better, it's just that you've found yourself, know better, and would rather do better. It's not that what you're wearing doesn't fit you, you don't look right, or you're naïve for the peculiar way that you think. It's just that you're dissimilar. You have your own style

that compliment your growth and is healthy for you.
Unfortunately, your parents, siblings and even your closest
friends will find that your distinguished personality is
intricate. This may have caused many of us to become
aghast of our differences. It's arduous for us to embrace our
unrelated characteristics when most of our parents treated
us analogous.

Back in July 2017, something occurred that left me
awestruck. My son was 8 years old at the time and seemed
bothered about something. We went from discussing what
he wanted to do for his 9th birthday, to me asking him what
was on his mind. Now when it come to my son, he is very
outgoing and intelligent. However, there's a silent introvert,
nonchalant stubborn side of him, as well.

With him being this way, it takes a lot to get him to
open and speak his mind. As we set in my living room, I
calmly suggested different things that could've been wrong.
Everything I could possibly think of wasn't the answer to
his built-up frustration. All he wanted to do was go to his
room and go to sleep. Now I could've said forget it and let
him continue to carry the burden. However, I realized that
2017 was a rough year for me.

I had just recently escaped from a demonic cult. I
was broken and damaged trying to cope spiritually,
mentally and emotionally. I was also occupied with running
my first daycare business and writing my first book. I
apologized to my son and explained to him that I was
concerned. For approximately 2 hours, I sat and watched as

he cried. He finally he decided to speak, "I feel like I'm a mistake. It's like I'm no different from anyone around me. I am, I know I am but what's the point of me being alive if I can't be myself. It's always about what you want, how you feel and what you think. What about me? It bothers me so much that it hurt. I just want to be myself. Let me dress myself and pick out items that I like. You may not like it but it's not about you. This is my life, not yours. Can you please just let me be myself? I don't know who I am, but I know that I'm not like everyone else. Can you let me decide and learn on my own?" he cried.

As tears flowed from my eyes, I apologized for making him feel like he was no different. I respected his feedback and granted his request. From that day forward, I allowed him to be himself. I stopped buying him what I liked, and I let him choose his own clothes/shoes.

Every day I allowed him to dress himself for school or when we went out in general. At times he would dress crazy and it irritated me. I'd rather him feel comfortable being himself, then to feel uncomfortable being who I felt he should be. Take a moment and think about what I just shared. Are you going through something similar or did you already cross this bridge? Now try to picture your neighborhood. What do you see? Does everyone look the same to you or not? Same hair, shoes, and clothes. If anyone should be caught without the same thing as everyone else, have you ever noticed that it becomes a problem?

I want to start off by saying, it all starts at home first. In most cases, whatever we teach our children, most of them will plant and reproduce throughout the world. If we choose to continuously lack knowledge, there's a possibility that our children may do the same. This will lead them to feed off others in the environment, causing them to be competitive and a counterfeit of everyone they come across.

A competitive individual is lost and unidentified simply searching for their identity. They go around feeding off others to find themselves only to come out even more lost then before. Believe it or not, most of us and our children are either publicly or privately competitive. This explains why most of our children and other people children are dying at such a young age.

Everyday you turn on the news or simply look out your window, you see/hear about another teenager or child that's been killed over something so foolish. All it takes is for one individual to not know who they are, for all hell to break loose. They will get involved with others who feel the same and before you know it, conflict will arouse. With this going on, most of our children will slowly begin to drop like flies.

If our children aren't damaging themselves, they may carry, hold hate and anger within them. This may lead them to unintentionally abuse another individual. They will find a way to bully and beat down anyone who is different. They will find a way to demolish anyone who refuse to partake in the same activities. In most cases, they grow into confused adults trying to keep up with everything and everybody. They're unstable, insecure and indecisive about everything. This is not fair at all, yet this is what occurs when we teach our children that they aren't distinguished, they're analogous.

I know you may think that I am taking this way out of proportion. However, try not to underestimate the minor things in life. Within a blink of an eye, those minor things can turn out to be extremely major and out of your reach. As a parent, I came to realization that both my children were created by God and I was used by God to birth them. Until this day, when I look at them, I can see their differences. Now I understand that God created them differently to fulfill his purpose.

I had to ask myself, If God created them differently who am I to treat them the same? I learned to treat them accordingly, yet my love for them both will always remain the same. I say all this to say this, try to stop treating your children the same. Not only should you embrace their differences but teach them how. Start now while you still can and understand that it's never too late. Get to know your children individually and allow them to be redeemed. Break the dysfunctional generational cycle that's been operating incorrectly for years, in which most of us have become adjusted too.

Let's teach our children how to come together using their differences to change the world. Let's also teach them how to embrace their differences to become a better person each day. Just think about it…the reason the same things keep occurring is because we do what we see and not what we know we should be doing. What we should be doing stands out separately yet joins together as one in the end.

There are different kinds of service, but we serve the same Lord.

-1 Corinthians 12:5NLT

Remember it all starts at home first. Are you making a difference for your children sake? or are you allowing the "same" to hinder your children while making them feel as if they're no different?

Chapter 5: Provide

Not too long ago, I was having a conversation with my mother. We discussed a situation regarding my 16-year old sister. Now at 16 years old, you and I both know there's a lot of peer pressure going on. Peer pressure is not only at school, it's all around even at home. In this time of day, the things that are occurring at home and school will drive a teenager insane. Honestly, I can understand why depression, mental illness and suicidal thoughts are at its highest peak.

In these days, if you're caught dressing a certain way than what others expect, people judge you. It's almost like you really don't have a choice. Most people find themselves suffering from fitting in and being popular. It's tough when all you want to do is standout by moving in the opposite direction of the crowd. Now on top of being an honor student, this explains what my sister is struggling with.

While trying to explain this to my mother, her response left me awestruck.

"Listen Shamika, that girl is crazy. I don't have time to be dealing with this, I have to go to work. If I don't go to work, explain to me who gone take care of me? since you know it all. You steady saying she's going through this and that, how? when she don't work. She don't provide and pay the bills around here, I do. I don't have time for this, all she needs to do is go to school. That's all she needs to be worried about".

Before I proceed and explain to you why this was my mother reaction/response, I would like for you to think back for a moment. When I ask you to think back throughout the book, I don't want you to feel like I'm trying to bring your past into the future. That's impossible. However, it's alright to look back to examine what was wrong so you can make it right, if you can, while moving forward.

Now as a child, have your parents every responded to you in such way? They may not have expressed it verbally, however, have you noticed it within their actions?

Most of our parents, actions clearly revealed to us that they didn't have time for us. All they had time to do was work, pay the bills, provide our personal needs such as; roof over our head, food to eat, clothes/shoes and everything else that had a price on it. There is absolutely nothing wrong with this way of providing because as a parent this is what's supposed to get done. The problem occurs when most of our parents only practiced what they were supposed to do and not what they needed to do.

The things that they need to do plays a bigger role than what they're supposed to do, the only difference is it's priceless. It's amazing how the things that comes priceless are the most difficult to give. I know that may sound crazy but it's the truth. The things that cost, in most cases, most can't even afford. We still break our neck trying to give it and prove points with no meaning to our children. Eventually what costs will fade away but what's priceless remains forever. This explains why most of us as children, who are now parents, are still angry and never fully satisfied.

Most of our parents have been taught to provide what they're suppose to and not what's needed. From generation to generation, we've been repeating the same dysfunctional affective cycle. All we know is what we've been taught by actions. Now from what we've been taught we pass down to our children. We're numb to how it made us feel and afraid to step up. Most of us have gotten so comfortable that we refuse to put an end to this disease. We know what we know, and most of us limit our ability to gain knowledge, learn, let go and grow.

Not everything that we know as parents is discombobulated, yet we only know bit and pieces. Most of us are comfortable with only knowing one way. There are many ways and techniques to be the best parent you know how to be. After an extended period, most of us settle and give up on knowledge, this affects our children because whatever we don't know, in most cases they won't know as well.

My people are destroyed for lack of knowledge. Because you have rejected knowledge, I also will reject you from being priest for Me; Because you have forgotten the law of your God, I also will forget your children.

-Hosea 4:6NKJV

I know for a fact the last thing you would want is your children finding out anything in these deceived, coldhearted streets. When we provide what we're suppose to, we teach our children to do the same thing. We leave them unaware of understanding how to provide what's needed. In many ways, we shape their way of thinking to believe what's needed to be provided is not important. Most of us parents, confuse our children by doing what we're suppose to do while using that as an excuse. We make them feel like we're providing what's needed as well.

For Example: Some parents stress to their children that because they pay the rent, keep a roof over their head, buy video games/babies dolls, and took them out to amusement parks; they love and care deeply for them. However, we wonder why our children never seem to be buoyant. We wonder why their always infuriated with us and grow to resent us while isolating themselves from us.

I remember when my eldest son was 4 years old. During this time, he was my only child, so I spoiled him. Bi-weekly when I got paid, I made sure he had 2 pairs of Jordan, Nikes, numerous outfits, toys and games. He would be excited temporary, then he would start back looking angry and irritated. I would ask him what's wrong, but he never said anything. This caused me to get frustrated because I felt like I was doing everything right. It seemed as if none of this stuff mattered to him. I had my times where I would yell and demand him to get his attitude together. I explained to him that there is no reason he should be looking/acting the way he was. I figured he should be excited eternally, based off the materialistic things I brought him.

I responded this way towards him up until he was 6 years old, then I stopped. It had dawned on me that my son felt, similar to, when I was a child. He was affected on the inside by the things that needed to be provided such as; attention, love, communication, nurture, guidance and discipline. It wasn't that I didn't have time. It was that I didn't know how to provide those priceless, substantial life essentials.

I went by what I seen my mother do and I became adjusted to it. I refuse to seek God for correction, guidance and knowledge to learn how to provide such things. To be completely honest, I didn't have any knowledge of God. It wasn't until my mid-20s that I begin to seek God. I know you're probably like, why didn't she just ask her mother? why did she seek God? Once a child is grown and out on their own, their parents still may not know. Based off my experience, I realized the best way to survive and live with a clear understanding of what life holds, is to seek God for everything. I've learned and I'm still learning that he is the only one that know everything.

Nothing in all creation is hidden from God. Everything is naked and exposed before his eyes, and he is the one to whom we are accountable.

-Hebrews 4:13NLT

Moving forward, I explained all of this to my mother. I asked her to try and take a different approach then she normally would, for my sister sake. Incontinently, she got frustrated. As a child, have you ever asked your parent a question or talked about something that was important to you? What was their response/reaction? I ask because some parents are impatient and can get very irritated with whatever the child finds interesting to discuss.

This makes the child feel as if they're a problem to the parent. It's not that the parent is irritated by the child, it's just that the parent would rather avoid a lot of questions. They'd rather not get wrapped up in discussions because in most cases, they don't know the answers. Most parents are not willing to make time to listen or learn about anything outside of what they already know. The more a person learn, the more accountable they become. This explains why a lot of people are comfortable with lacking knowledge.

I'm sure most of us experienced this with our parents. I'm sure our children have experienced this, with us as well. At times we can't help but to react in which we've been reacted to. We can't help but to teach in which what's been taught to us. Most of us refuse to take that extra step, and it's not always because of fear. It's simply because that extra step wasn't taken for us.

Most of us parents, will literally place our time and effort in providing what we're suppose to. We resist placing that same effort and time in providing what our children need the most. As I continued the conversation with my mother, she then, suggested that my sister speak with a counselor. Here is another issue that I noticed most parents practice. They go and hire maids, counselors, tutors, and nannies. They pay that extra money so someone else can provide what their child needs.

If only they had enough patience to cast all their cares upon God and focus strictly on him, things would be much better. God has the power to teach all of us what we need to know, correct what we thought we knew and teach/show us what we never knew. He will breakdown and empty us of the dysfunctional information we've been taught and rebuild us all. He will overflow us with his wisdom, knowledge and understanding. If we ask with pure motives and if it's according to his will, he will grant it.

Keep on asking, and you will receive what you ask for. Keep on seeking, and you will find it. Keep on knocking, and the door will be opened to you. For everyone who asks, receives. Everyone who seeks, finds. And to everyone who knocks, the door will be opened. -Matthew 7:7-8NLT

And even when you ask, you don't get it because your motives are all wrong-you only want what will give you pleasure. -James 4:3NLT

However, God will never force us as parents to seek him and gain knowledge from him. We should freely choose to accept it and not limit our ability to present it. If you look around a lot of us resent our parents. Most of us brag about what our parents are supposed to do, we say:

"Momma did what she had to do. It was a lot of us and only her. She was a hard worker".

Do you see how we make up excuses and make an idol out of the wrong things? To be completely honest, what most of our parents did is what they chose to do. If they chose to have multiple children back to back, and work 5 jobs, that was their choice. This shouldn't justify why they failed to provide what we needed the most. Why were most of us left suffering the consequences of their decisions? Anything a person does, never just affects them, it affects everyone around them as well. I say this quite often because if you think about it, it's true.

Whether or not we want to accept and admit it, most of our children suffer for the very same reasons. From this day forward, lets try to be a greater generation of parents. Let us not continue to resent, hold on to unforgiveness, blame our parents for what they didn't do and repeat their ways. Let us no longer be deceived or afraid. When it come to our childhood memories, let us begin to remember. Let us go back to the root of it all, so that we can gain knowledge and have patience to provide what's needed, for our children sake.

Chapter 6: Mistakes and Losing

In this time of day, when we as parents make a mistake, we tend to belittle ourselves. Most of us feel ashamed, embarrassed and disqualified. We put on this perfect strength and mask to show our children, we got this. Most of us walk around disguised as if we're winning on the outside, yet we're losing on the inside. I understand that we desire the best life for our children.

I understand that we try to be a living example but lately, most of us have been a lying example. What do I mean by that? Lately we've been putting on a show without first rehearsing it. We've been teaching our children by our actions that making mistakes and losing is not an option. For an extended period, most of us act as if mistakes and losing is a sign of weakness, disqualification and failure.

We teach by our actions that if you make a mistake, you're not strong or smart enough. When we, our children or another individual lose, most of us feel like we'll never be enough to win, so we give up. I understand the strive that we all have within us to keep winning, keep moving and never stop. Even if it's draining and we're exhausted from it, we still do it.

Now I am not saying that there's something wrong with winning, this is not the issue. The issue occurs when we as parents, fail to teach our children that there are lessons, blessings, and growth that comes from mistakes and losing. What most of us fail to realize is that our imperfections is what slowly shape us into perfection. When we continue to put on a mask and broadcast a counterfeit strength, we lie, mislead and confuse our children.

Most of us continuously raise them up this way. This cause them to strive much harder than they should. They become adjusted in winning all the time that when they lose, they can't seem to understand why. Once again, when they don't realize that they've lost; they become blinded to the lessons, blessings and the chance to grow.

Think about a time or two when you kept losing or even made numerous mistakes. What was your response to the situation? After so many times of losing and constant mistakes, most of us start feeling like what's the point. We stop putting effort into the situation that we're trying to continuously win in. Negative thoughts and depression creeps in and we begin to settle, doubt and allow it to overtake us.

I want you to take a moment and try to understand that for every lost and mistake you've ever encountered, did not take place because you're incapable. It didn't occur for you to give up. It didn't happen because you're not fit to succeed and be a winner. That mistake you made and lost you had to take was a lesson in which you needed to learn to obtain growth in that area. It occurred so that you

42

can prosper properly as you exceed and proceed forward in your life.

When most of us are winning and hit rock bottom, we try to immediately get back on top. Rarely, do we start over from the bottom to examine ourselves. Rarely, do we figure out where and why exactly did the mistake or lost take place to begin with. We don't set aside time to figure out the root of the cause. Instead, we just keep on damaging ourselves trying to win.

If we continue to be ashamed of our imperfections, our ability to learn from them, grow and move forward, may be hindered. As parents our actions will show our children to never express but forever hide their imperfections. This may cause them to think that losing is not an option and the only way, is to win. This may also cause them to be overly independent, afraid to make mistakes and/or ask for help. This may even cause them to repeatedly take on more than they can labor.

Examining and understanding the mistakes you made, will eternally place you in a position to succeed in life. God desires for us and our children to win and be successful in everything we do. Without mistakes, losing, hardships, and faith; most of us will continue to remain in a season that repeats the same things.

This is only until we learn properly how to become stable enough, to fix what we can and accept what we can't. During our winning season, a lot of things can creep in without recognizing. Things such as; pride, greed, jealousy, envy, lust, low self-esteem, anger, selfishness, and frustration. These things can be overwhelming and a big distraction. These things are also the reason why we're running the race at our best speed, yet always seem to fail. Somehow, we still can't seem to win even after we finally touched the finish line.

These distractions are not an option of whether we want to deal with them or not. The way they creep in, most of us rarely notice them. This explains why it's mandatory to be aware and spot them every chance we get. In most cases, a lot of these things will overtake us, and this will cause us to lose. It will cause us to miss out on what we didn't catch the first, second and maybe third time around. This is amazing because you get another chance to get things in order the next time around.

For Example: Back in your school days, (elementary, high school and/or college) when you took a substantial test and failed it, what did you do? Did you immediately retake the test due to frustration of your grade? or did you examine the test to see where you went wrong at, even after studying tremendously? Most of us, take the test without examination and still fail. Most of us, examine where we went wrong, accept it, learn from it, fix it, then we pass the test, successfully.

So, you see… when you lose, it's like you win again and come back better, depending on how you go about things. This explains why, there is absolutely nothing wrong with mistakes or losing. As parents, lets begin to be a real example of what it really means to win. Let us not only show by actions but let us discuss the benefits that can and will be reaped from the mistakes and loses that comes with life.

By doing this, our children won't be so angry or ashamed when they make a mistake or fail. We won't be infuriated and feel that are children aren't good enough as well. Instead, we will all benefit from what we lost at. We will be able to learn, grow, change, and forgive, in every opportunity we get whether we're exceeding or failing.

Chapter 7: Living and Surviving

Growing up have you ever seen your parents live? Did they ever go for a walk to the park? Maybe spend a day at the lakefront to breathe? Perhaps, they went to an art gallery to bring out the creativeness placed within them. Did you ever see your parents live? Do you know what it means to live? Before I proceed, think about this question: Are you living your life or are you surviving life? I know you're probably like it's the same thing, it's all life. However, there's a big difference between the two.

Nowadays, what we see, most of us assume then we repeat the same things. I know it may seem as if this has just started, yet it hasn't. This is something that has been going on for years now from generation to generation. The only difference is that it has gotten worse. Growing up, many of us have been taught to simply survive. What exactly do I mean by that? Well, we've been taught and programmed to go to school, stay in school, graduate and get a good paying job.

Most of us have heard our parents say this repeatedly. Due to us not knowing who we are, we figured they knew what they were talking about. Even if we've never seen them practice what they preach, we still believe them, and we still do it. Have your parents ever told you to seek God first in everything you do and everything else will fall into place?

Seek the Kingdom above all else and he will give you everything you need.

-Luke 12:31NLT

Did your parents ever express to you to focus strictly on God, so that you can find your identity and purpose? Were they a living example of what they kept trying to get you to understand?

Back in Chapter 6, I explained to you that most of our parents blocked their ability to gain knowledge. They know what they know regardless if it's wrong. Most of them limit themselves from further comprehension. Most of them lack knowledge, then grow bitter and have many regrets. They believe they don't have a second chance to better themselves and get back on the path God paved for them. They believe that their regrets are wisdom. They share it with you, hoping that you would listen so they can live again through you.

The crazy part about all of this is that they're capable themselves, they just stop believing. Most of them never lived to establish their identity and purpose. They lived long enough to survive. I just want you to know that their life was theirs and yours, is yours. God created us all filled with something different that would bring glory to his name. I say this because a lot of our parents would try to be controlling, using us to live for them. The only one that's able to live through us and use us, is the one whom created us, God.

Most of our parents may have lived to see 60 and older, may be deceased, or still maybe alive. However, they died back in their early 20s, or mid-30s. What do I mean by that? They limited, gave up, settled, and stop believing in themselves at that age. Most of them lacked knowledge. This caused them to use every day opportunities given, to remain regretful and bitter. They then, became adjusted to doing just enough that's needed to survive.

Most of them became so numb to surviving that they didn't understand that a new day brings new opportunities. When our parents and even ourselves refuse to seek God for our identity, change, growth and purpose; we become confused and discouraged. We then, unconsciously pass down the dysfunction to the next generation, which is our children. I understand that when you're trying to succeed, the idea of giving God a drop of your time is way too much. I am also aware that it's difficult believing what you can't see.

I've learned overtime that the things I felt was too much, wasn't much at all. I dropped everything and let God in for a change. I also learned that truly surrendering all to God, was the solution to all my worries and problems. From there on I began to live.

Those who look to him for help will be radiant with joy; no shadow of shame will darken their faces. In my desperation I prayed, and the Lord listened; he saved me from all my troubles.

-Psalms 34:5-6NLT

I say all this to say, until we seek God for our identity and purpose, we will forever remain in a survival mode. Survival mode is a dangerous place to be in. It's like you're alive but you're not living. If you've practiced surviving long enough, it will put you in a place where you will only do what you're suppose to do to get by. If you look around most of us are stuck in survival mode. I say we're stuck because the thought of living seems to terrify us.

We're either sitting around waiting on someone else to help us survive or we're doing it alone. Most of us think to live is to go out to the club, get high, and drink every weekend. However, that's really a temporary break we take from surviving. During times like this we're just having fun. We're not in our right state of mind to think clearly. This is something most of us do to clear our mind temporary but it's not enough to live permanently. Just think about when you're back sober again. Life still awaits you to live and be free.

A lot of us are afraid of what we don't know. I know this may sound awkward but it's the truth.

For Example: Most of us are afraid to live because we don't know how to live, neither do we know what living comes with. We're glad to settle with just surviving because not only are we comfortable but that's all we've been taught to do. Think about this question as you continue to read: Now that you are grown with children and a family of your own, do you have to continue to pass down what you've been taught? Especially if you know it was unhealthy and unfair.

I know you may think that's all you know, yet there is so much awaiting you to learn and continue to grow. Now if your parents were fair and taught you well, this doesn't pertain to you. If not, think about how it caused you to isolate and belittle yourself. Think about all the times you may have thought about are you worthy enough to live a meaningful, abundant, and prosperous life.

Most of us devalue ourselves and refuse to live. We choose to survive day after day. If we're not careful those around us, perhaps, our children, will pick up our energy and produce the same habits. They will only know how to survive, and they may not feel worthy enough to live their own lives.

For Example: If you look around most of our children are growing up in grammar school, off to high school and just about done with college. Most of the things that they're majoring and may even graduate for, they never seem to fulfill. What do I mean by that? They may receive the degree, but they gave up pursing the purpose. What they see and is programmed to believe sticks close and overrides their natural born purpose. If they continue to stay in

50

survival mode, there's a possibility they may not establish their purpose that occurs from living.

I'm sure you've noticed your child gifts and talents. They may have grown and practiced these things on the side. Due to you not embracing it at that moment, they're afraid to let it be known. They're also unaware of how to embrace and accept it. They don't take what flows naturally serious and the say they're good at it, but it doesn't pay the bills.

Our children don't understand that if they remain faithful in pursuing their purpose, they will never have to worry about the cares of this life.

Think about the things of heaven, not the things of earth. For you died to this life and your real life is hidden with Christ in God. And when Christ, who is your life, is revealed to the whole world, you will share in all his glory.

-Colossians 3:2-4NLT

Most of them don't understand because most of us didn't understand. It wasn't learned not only because it wasn't taught but because we failed to learn for our children's sake. Once again, we can't base our ability to learn and grow off what we were and weren't taught. As parents, we are held accountable to learn and accept knowledge for not only our children, but for ourselves as well. Once more, what we lack, our children we also lack until either we change that or until they grow older and decide to no longer lack knowledge.

Moving forward, I know you're probably stunned and wondering at this point how do you get out of survival mode and begin to live. First and foremost, seek God so that he can enliven you in every area. He will shine his light on those dark, rooted affected areas within you. This will help most of us accept and face ourselves. As we examine ourselves, we will begin to think. Thinking is a good thing. It allows you to open slowly and gravitate towards knowledge.

Once you start learning, nothing can block your growth and ability to continue learning. When you grow, you're more aware of those things in which you once were blind to. You're able to modify and embrace the change within you that you've always desired to come about. Change is amazing because it gives you the opportunity to exceed and proceed in life. You will begin to understand that it's impossible for a change to occur if you ever decided to settle.

This all will lead you down the path that God destined for you to begin with. It will not be effortless. It will take a lot of patience; however, it will be worth it. I just want you to know that in everything you succeed in, settling shouldn't be apart of it. In fact, it's impossible to settle and live. You can settle and survive but you can't settle and live. So, in order to live you should try to;

-Seek God and surrender all to God

-Think about the consequences before making any decisions.

-Be honest as you learn, accept, examine and face yourself (it's never too late to start)

-Grow repeatedly and never let yourself or anyone else hinder your growth.

-Embrace and be open for change. Understand that nothing will ever change around you, until a change takes place within you.

Once we practice these simple, yet difficult steps, we will begin to live. The things we were taught that was dysfunctional and left most of us discombobulated, will no longer matter. The things we learn from seeking God matters and will last forever. Remember, there is no settling in forever. If we want our children to live life abundantly, we should be a living example of what it means to live. We should at least try to stop reciprocating the cycle of what it means to survive.

No degree or steep paying job will ever be able to exceed the seed that's been placed within you. -Shamika King

Chapter 8: Attention

Do you pay attention to your children? If so, how often? Is it all the time or rarely? To be more specific, when I say pay attention, I don't mean telling your child how much they look like their dad or how great of a job they did on their homework. That's more of a compliment or giving attention. Most of us don't understand the distinguished concept of paying and giving attention.

Perhaps, we've come to a place in our lives where we believe they are the same. By the Grace of God, I come to share with you and clear up any false accusations regarding the diverseness between the two. We can not practice one without the other. It may simply damage and disorient our children if we continue to misinterpret the two. Before I move forward, I would like to explain what Paying and giving attention means regarding the child.

Pay Attention

When you pay attention to your children, you're focus strictly on them. You're devoted to them and you can hear them loud and clear even when they're not speaking. You're concerned about them, not only physically but spiritually, emotionally and mentally. You know almost everything about them, and you don't get in the way of their growth. You're always observing ready to teach them as they exceed on new levels. Your vision is so clear you can see God's plan for them. You encourage them in every way to fulfill their destiny, without any pressure. You understand them so well that you can tell the difference between their *Likes, Goods and Natural Born Gift.*

You know when they're being dishonest and loyal. You also know when someone else is being dishonest and loyal regarding your child. You know when they're capable and incapable of achieving something, but you never discourage them. You let them learn, as you gradually help them without force, as they move forward. Just as much as you know these things about your child, your child can also detect if you understand or not. They can sense if you're paying attention to them or giving them attention to pass time.

Give Attention

When you give attention to your children, it's almost as if it's from a careless place. It's like you're there physically but you're absent in every other area.

For Example: When you attend your child school play or first game, majority of the time, you're on your phone. If not that, your mind dwells elsewhere. Just because you're in a certain place at a certain time, doesn't mean you're fully aware of what's going on.

As a lost child all grown up now into not only an adult but a parent, most of us have given up on our children simply by giving them attention. When you give your child attention, they may forever seek it. They may forever remain disheveled and irretrievable. Have your child ever asked you something? If so, what was your response? Did you examine and comprehend what they asked you about? Or did you give them attention, just enough to pretend like you care so they can get out of your sight?

I understand as a parent that you may still dwell on past hurt and memories. You may even be still on a search for someone to pay attention to you. Once again, the more you give attention to your child, the more your child may seek it. This may even cause them to grow selfish and never fully satisfied. Reason being is because you're simply giving unassured attention to what they want. You resist the root affect of what's needed when you refuse to pay attention.

When you pay attention, you can properly give attention. They both go hand and hand. One without the other may confuse and/or mislead your child.

From generation to generation, our parents and even we ourselves have been giving too much attention. We have become prone to giving the attention that it has blocked our ability to pay attention. Up until this day and so forth, most of us are still on a search for someone to simply pay attention to us. Most of us have been raised not knowing what attention is at all. This cause a lot of us to be used, manipulated and controlled by others who pretend to pay attention to us.

Since most of us have been raised not knowing the difference, up until this day we're still on the search for it. Not only did most of our parents, but we ourselves could never tell the difference between our *Likes, Goods and Natural Born Gift.* As you continue to read, I will explain *Likes, Goods and Natural Born Gift*. I will also explain how they differ.

Likes

Are numerous things that may grasp your child attention. Although they may be or seem interested, it's only temporary. After awhile your child will grow to like other things without finding anymore interest in their previous or past likes.

Goods

Are multiple subjects or hobbies that your child may be good at. They strike an interest within your child and your child study, tryout or practice at it. However, after a while, similar to likes, goods get to a point in your child's life, where it bores them. Your child maybe good at many different things, yet only for a short period of time.

Natural Born Gift

Is what has naturally been installed within your child. They don't like it and they aren't good at it. In fact, they love it and they're a genius at it. They are naturally equipped for it. It flows without force and the moment they lay their hands on it, it's like they've been doing it their entire life. Your child's natural born gift is bountiful and everlasting. It's amazing because although they're young, they're aware of it and desire to embrace and pursue it. It's permanent, and no matter what it never changes. It only gets better and multiply. The more it's nurtured properly, the more it blossoms.

Take a moment, think back as far as you can remember to your childhood. Have you ever concluded that, your own parents don't even know you? It's amazing how during the process of your growth, they try to give you attention without fully paying attention to you. What do I mean by that?

For Example: Your natural born gift never mattered simply because they didn't understand you. The only way to understand a child in general is to pay attention to them. Growing up, it's almost like you're forced to live your parent's life, due to their regrets and lack of knowledge. This causes them to get your *Likes, Goods, and Natural Born Gift* mixed up. Based off your likes and goods falling in the temporary category, this causes a decrease in the attention that most parents refused to pay.

When you give attention, you're not fully aware of what's going on. Now if you place likes, goods and giving attention all together, the similarities of them are all temporary. In most cases, what the child is good at can sometimes lead to their natural born gift but not all the time.

For Example: When your child present something that they like or good at to you, what is your reaction or response? More than rare, most parents respond unconsciously. We say, "Yup. Great! I think you should go for it." However, when it's their natural born gift, most parents think their children are crazy. They don't feel like the child natural born gift will bring in more money than working in the health field would. Most parents discourage their children by making them feel like that's not for them.

We give attention just to charge up our child to exit out of our presence. I'm unaware as to why but as parents most of us refuse to pay attention to our children and their natural born gift. This is unfair and unhealthy. In most cases, this explain why most children grow into unstable adults trying to be like everyone else. They think what they desire is what God created them to fulfil. However, no matter how much they accomplish, that unidentified, unperceived feeling lingers within them.

They find themselves seeking for anyone to simply pay them attention. They know if only someone could pay them attention maybe they will have a chance to find out their identity and fulfil their destiny. Again, this too is unhealthy and may damage the child. In this time of day, there are numerous predators that prey on children and adults, by presenting a counterfeit description of "Paying Attention". They pay attention to our children just to lead them astray and manipulate them. This may affect the child even more.

In most cases, our children transform into a trouble child. They see no point in living life and so they take life for granted. They start lying and getting into all kinds of conflict. They grow disrespectful, say and partake in foul activities. They not only grow disrespectful to you but to any form of authority or people in general. It can get so bad that most of us have to watch our children lose their innocent lives at such a young age.

We see it all the time. Almost every day, you would think something is in the air the way children are dropping left to right. Most parents cry and testify about how it's not right and they're right. However, it's not right or fair when the child is not being properly nurtured at home. It's not right when most parents refuse to pay attention to their children, then have the audacity to scream for justice. Justice starts at home first, not out in the environment when trouble occurs.

From this day forward, as a parent try to pay more attention to your children. I know you may be going through a lot yourself. I know you're probably still on a search for someone to pay attention to you, however, try to balance it out. Set aside some time every day if you can, to nurture your children with this life essential. Understand that just because they can't see it, doesn't mean that they're not aware of it. Just because they can't see it, doesn't mean they don't yearn for it, as it silently affects them.

Chapter 9: Balance

Throughout the book you have learned about what the child can't see affects them. You might've even learned some things that grasp your full attention. I don't want you to think that what the child can see, doesn't affect them because it does. At times, what goes on the outside adds on to that inner turmoil. As you read thoroughly through the chapters, I'm sure that I didn't catch you by surprise. In every chapter, if not everything, some things triggered within you.

I'm sure it took you back to a place that you left unannounced or hidden. I'm sure for a long time you may have felt that it doesn't matter, and it would never come up again. One thing I've learned is what you refuse to fix that needs to be fixed, will remain on hold and unfixed. It's almost like déjà vu when you watch your children reciprocate, react and reveal your inner secrets, in which, you never spoke about. Leaving the situation unresolved because you're afraid to face it, won't benefit you or your children.

What's manifested on the inside will eventually come out. Unintentionally, you may find yourself reciprocating what you've grown adjusted to and may have caused you to struggle. For most of us we'd rather take the easy way out and block out any signs of struggle. We don't like the thought of it. If it's a struggle to learn and gain knowledge, most of us run and would rather not deal with it. Just think about it, what would life be without a struggle? We may never be able to learn, grow and gain knowledge, we'd be stuck just like most of our parents. Until this day, believe it or not most of us are stuck as well.

Based off most of our history, we leave our children unaware of a lot of substantial things that would be beneficial to them. Before I proceed, think about the causes and effects that are rooted in areas that you lack and ignore, in which your child yearns deeply for?

In this day of age, most parents are only practicing 3 things that I spoke about in the previous chapters;

1. *Providing what they're supposed to*
2. *Giving attention*
3. *Surviving*

As for all the other things that matters, such as; proper communication, discipline, responsibility, differences, paying attention, providing what's needed, teaching our children how to live, mistakes/losing and balance, most of us lack. There is no balance, which explains why most of our children are affected, misled, unstable, and confused. We can no longer do a half job at raising our children. We sow a little into them but expect to reap a full harvest from them.

For every chapter in this book, I ask that you try to understand that one cannot be done without the other. We can't continuously communicate without discipline. We can't expect our children to be different if we fail to pay attention to them. We can't expect them to be responsible, without first explaining the blessings and lessons that comes from losing and making mistakes.

Now although you can't do one without the other, you must be careful, why? Because you don't want to do too much but just enough. What do I mean by not doing too much but just enough? Take a moment and think back to when your child was a newborn baby. During this stage, you were assigned precise instructions on how to nurture and nourish your baby. Due to the baby being newly born, you can only do just enough but not too much. Feeding the baby too much formula will cause it to get sick, vomit or may even lead to death.

Holding the baby too much will make him/her spoiled. This will cause many problems, and no one will want to keep or be around the baby. This explains why you should practice balance, doing just enough and not too much, at the proper time. Now as your child get older, the level of nurturing will change, in fact, it's supposed to change. There won't be anymore formula, bottles, pampers, pacifiers, and baby talk. Although it shouldn't be any more, don't be surprised if you still witness or see this happening today. If you're still seeing this, just be aware that somewhere there's a lack of discipline, fear of growth, and a lack of balance

As parents, I know it's hard for us to watch our babies grow into adults. In our eyes they will forever be our babies and that's true, they will. However, we should move accordingly to their level of growth and be ready to nurture them. We should be prepared to balance out how we teach, convey, chasten, pay attention and escort them. Some of us parents are either doing too much of one thing or we're only balanced in one area of all things.

I understand that being a parent is not easy at all. It has its pros and cons, yet it's worth it. It's worth it when you take the time out to equip and encourage your child to be a better person and live their destined life. As a parent, I'm not asking for you to be perfect. I'm asking that you try not to be afraid to let your imperfections flow as you balance the way you raise your children.

Moving forward, I would like to explain 3 things that most parents fail to realize and practice for their children's sake.

1. *Unprepared- We're unprepared for our children to grow up and depart from us. We're afraid to let them go out in the world and get a dose of it, similar to the way we had to, in order to learn.*

2. *Standstill- We remain on a standstill and refuse not to nurture and feed our children knowledge due to us not being prepared. We sit back selfishly and watch our*

children reciprocate our history from generation to generation. It's sad and unfair to our children that we don't even have the words to say, due to us failing to gain as much knowledge as possible, so at some point in our lives we can be able to guide and lift them up in times of trouble.

3. *Updated- If we continue to practice one and two of what I just explained, we will not be able to properly keep our children updated. Keeping our children updated is very important, especially in this time of day. Anything you don't share with them or explain to them to be aware of, they will falsely find out elsewhere and it may be too late for them to learn from it.*

I'm sure you hear a lot of parents express how they don't trust anyone with their children. They don't even trust their children to go to the park, the movies or shopping at the mall. They think that this overprotection is a sign of love and compassion. However, it's not. If you truly love your child, you'd nurture, discipline, and balance out everything you teach them. If you truly love your child, you'd trust God enough to know that no matter what, your child will be in good hands at all times.

When any parent acts this way 9x's out of 10, it's because of something rooted within them from their past childhood. They probably never spoke about it with the child or they probably did but still refuse to let the child live. To prevent what they think may occur, out of fear of what happened to them, they keep the child converged. This to is another sign of lack of knowledge and a lack of balance within the parent. Once again, it's not because they don't know, it's because they choose not to know out of fear of the unknown. They also may have never taken the time out to learn because once they learn they become accountable. At times accountability can be too much of a struggle.

In all, this explains why there is no balance. Most parents are still holding on to a lot of things that's blocking their growth. If it's blocking their growth, it may block the child's growth. I always say what the parent don't know, the child won't know. Now if the child refuses to pass down the maladjusted cycle to their children, that's different. I just want you to know that a lot of what you see today started at home first before it was reproduced into the world.

I know you're probably wondering with all of what you just read about, how do you balance out the way you raise your child? Just be on top and aware of everything that your children need and yearn for the most. Feed them knowledge accordingly, just a little bit at a time. Share everything you learn with them and listen to what they share with you, daily. Try not to think that just because they're a child they don't need to know. This explains why people of all kinds prey on children first because the child is innocent, not updated, and not aware of what's happening.

I always say it's never too late to start but never take advantage of the time you start. When you start early you will never have to worry about whether it's too late. Keep this in mind for your children's sake. In everything you do regarding your children, make sure you're not getting in the way of their growth. Balance out all the life essentials that they yearn for without allowing your history to get in the way.

What They Can't See Affects Them   Shamika King

Special Letter to Reader

I want to thank you so much for taking the time out to read my book. I pray it was something said that touched your heart, opened your perception, and encouraged you to make a change for the better so forth. Nothing that I've written about is to offend or shame you. Every word was written from no other place than my heart. I thank God for consistently pouring into me because it gives me numerous opportunities to pour into you.

For everything that you've read and learned throughout this book, please understand that it is not my intentions to make you feel forced to do anything I spoke about. Always remember, if it's forced the outcome will never be right. As you slowly digest every word, take as much time as you need to activate, implement, and practice it daily.

Continue being the best you know how to be without bearing burdens and dwelling on the mess in which you use to be. Thank you so much and know that I don't write for myself, it's a gift from God for me to reciprocate to you.

I don't speak on my own authority. The Father who sent me has commanded me what to say and how to say it. -John 12:49

Contact Information

Podcast: Anchor.fm/nourishinspirations

<u>Other books by Shamika King</u>

Face Yourself

But God Kept Me

Nourish Inspirations

*All books are available on **amazon.com/author/shamikaking***

What They Can't See Affects Them   Shamika King

What They Can't See Affects Them   Shamika King

Made in the USA
Middletown, DE
08 June 2022

66757351R00050